Rock Being different!

Dawn

9 NOVEMBER 2018

Thank you Mom,

for encouraging me to be different.

www.mascotbooks.com

Being Different Rocks!

©2018 Dawn Michele McCarty. All Rights Reserved. No part of this publication may be reproduced, stored in a retrieval system or transmitted in any form by any means electronic, mechanical, or photocopying, recording or otherwise without the permission of the author.

For more information, please contact:
Mascot Books
620 Herndon Parkway #320
Herndon, VA 20170
info@mascotbooks.com

Library of Congress Control Number: 2017959402

CPSIA Code: PRT0418A
ISBN-13: 978-1-68401-254-1

Printed in the United States

BEING DIFFERENT ROCKS!

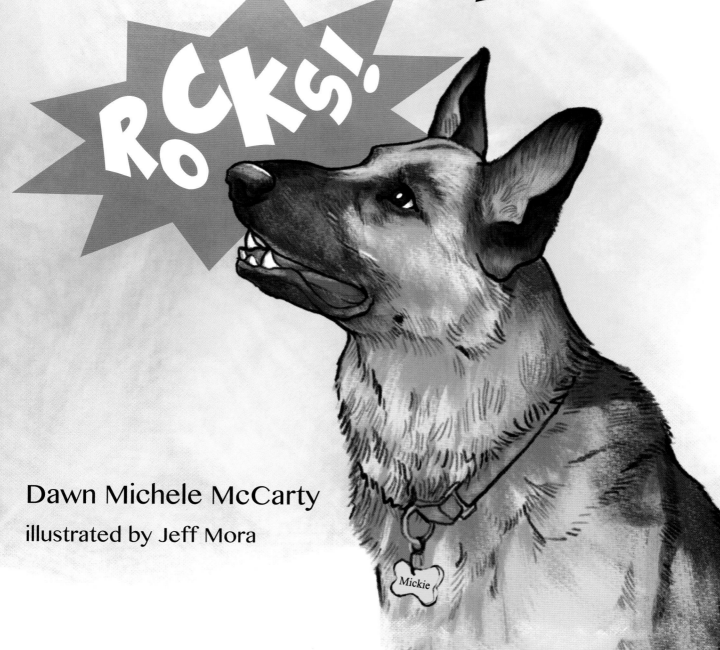

Dawn Michele McCarty

illustrated by Jeff Mora

Hi, my name is Mickie-D and I'm a German Shepherd. I was born at a dog breeder's. A breeder is a person who raises dogs to sell them.

But I wasn't for sale, because I was born different.

My feet are not like other dogs' feet. They look like short skis, and I make a lot of noise when I walk. Sometimes, I even trip.

THWACK-
THWACK-
THWACK

My feet will always be like this. They make me different. I don't mind them, but at the breeder's it meant that I was left to myself a lot.

No one played with me. I spent my days in a kennel watching the other dogs go home with families.

One day, a lady came and took me for a ride. I thought she was taking me to the vet for shots. Yuck!

But she treated me in a new way. She gave me great ear scratches and told me I was going to join a rescue family. I didn't know what that meant, but I liked her, so I was excited to find out.

She took me to a house, and I was allowed inside! I'd never been in a house before, so I didn't know what to do, but the lady told me it was safe to explore.

I smelled everything, climbed on everything, and even stuck my nose in the garbage! The lady laughed and said I would learn what I could and could not climb and smell in the house. No matter how good garbage smells, it's not for dogs. Darn!

Over time, I learned commands like sit, down, stay, and come. I learned to walk on a leash and the proper way to meet dogs and cats. My rescue family took me on adventures to pet stores and parks and on long walks.

I was amazed that my rescue family wanted to teach me even though sometimes I tripped over my long feet. But then I learned that a rescue is a group of people who volunteer to help others, both people and animals. I was lucky to have my very own rescue family.

One day, my rescue family took me to a specialist to examine my feet. She looked at them and said, "Yes, they're different, but he can do most anything other dogs can do."

I already knew that was true, but it was nice to hear.

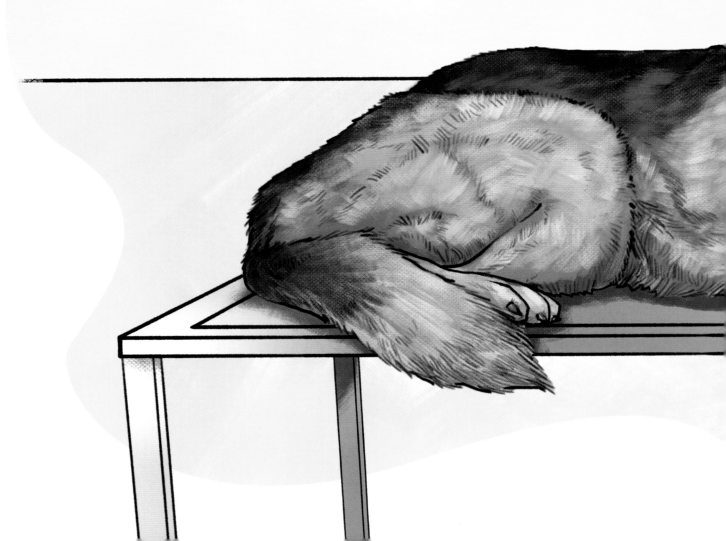

After that, I went to many events where families who had been approved to adopt from the rescue came to meet us.

Lots of people talked to me and visited me, but no one wanted to take me home.

One day, my rescue family told me that a couple was going to come to an event to meet me! They had been reading about me and following my story on the rescue's website. They lived in a house with lots of space to play, and best of all, they had been approved to be adoptive parents!

They had even waited to be approved before meeting me in person in case another family was lucky and adopted me first. I couldn't believe they thought whoever adopted me would be lucky!

When they came to the event, we spent a couple hours together and I really liked them. They even called me "perfect." Perfect? No one ever called me perfect.

"PERFECT?"

My foster mom decided I should visit their home. They had three other dogs so it was important I met them too. I couldn't wait! Was I going to have adoptive parents and siblings, too?

FUREVER FAMILY

Finally, the day came for the visit. I only waited a week, but it seemed like forever. When we arrived at their home, I met each dog one at a time. I liked them all!

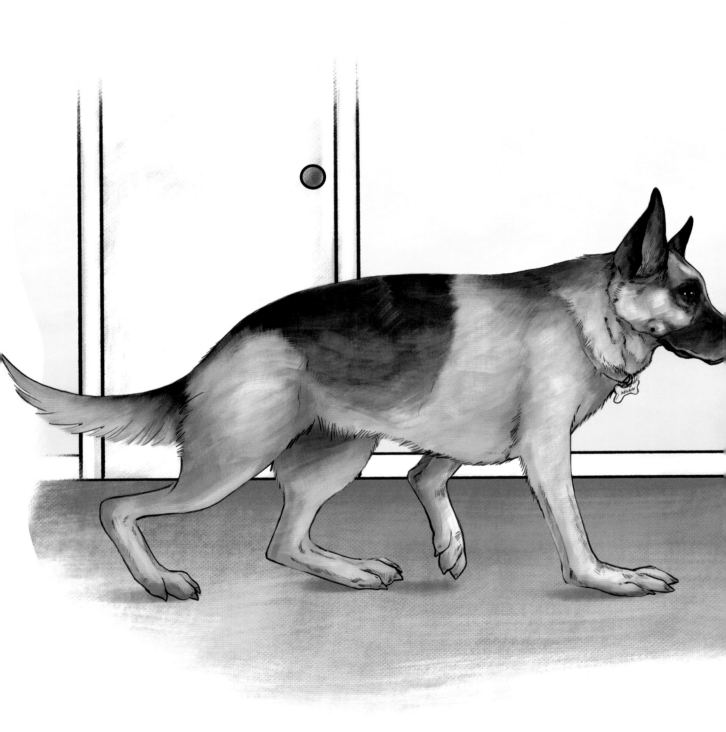

I explored their home and all the new smells. They had stairs, which were tricky at first for my funny feet, but they had put carpet on the stairs for me. I conquered them in no time!

Next, we went for a walk. The family's yard was big with lots of trees and a walking trail with a creek behind it. My funny feet took me down the trail and into the creek, no problem! I even kept up with my three new friends. We had a blast!

After a few hours, my foster mom said it was obvious that I was home.

Now, I spend my days playing with my brothers, walking in the woods, practicing my commands—you never stop learning—playing games, and going on short runs. Yup, I can run! My parents tell me I can do anything I want and they're right. My feet may be different, but that doesn't limit me. In fact, they're better than my brothers' feet in the snow. I don't sink at all!

I used to be sad and hurt when people said I was different, not normal, or strange looking. Now I know that being different ROCKS!

Virginia German Shepherd Rescue (VGSR)

VGSR was started in 2001 by a small group of individuals dedicated to rescuing, rehabilitating, and rehoming German Shepherd Dogs. Since 2001, over 4,000 dogs have been rescued and found their furever homes thanks to the dedication and commitment of volunteers giving their love, time, talents, and energy. To learn more about VGSR's mission, please visit www.vgsr.org.

Mickie

Thanks to the efforts of VGSR volunteers, Mickie was surrendered to the rescue and started a new adventure. Mickie was very special and it was not because of his feet. He was a fabulous companion who knew when I was having a less than terrific day and would lay next to me and let me curl up on him. Mickie was not a dog who liked being hugged, but knew when I needed it. Mickie enjoyed playing with his canine pals and napping with his feline buddies. Trail walking was a favorite pastime of Mickie's. Mickie also loved playing in the snow and catching snowballs that I would launch at him. He made me laugh every day and will always be in my heart.

— Dawn